www.penguin.co.uk

Jane Austen's Hilarious Guide to Ghosting, Courtships and Bagging Your Mr Darcy

Satu Hämeenaho-Fox

bantam

TRANSWORLD PUBLISHERS
UK | USA | Canada | Ireland | Australia
India | New Zealand | South Africa

Transworld is part of the Penguin Random House group of companies whose addresses can be found at global.penguinrandomhouse.com.
Penguin Random House UK, One Embassy Gardens, 8 Viaduct Gardens, London SW11 7BW
penguin.co.uk

Penguin Random House UK

First published in Great Britain in 2025 by Bantam
an imprint of Transworld Publishers

001

Copyright © Satu Hämeenaho-Fox 2025

The moral right of the author has been asserted

This book is a work of fiction and, except in the case of historical fact, any resemblance to actual persons, living or dead, is purely coincidental.

Every effort has been made to obtain the necessary permissions with reference to copyright material, both illustrative and quoted. We apologize for any omissions in this respect and will be pleased to make the appropriate acknowledgements in any future edition.

Penguin Random House values and supports copyright. Copyright fuels creativity, encourages diverse voices, promotes freedom of expression and supports a vibrant culture. Thank you for purchasing an authorized edition of this book and for respecting intellectual property laws by not reproducing, scanning or distributing any part of it by any means without permission. You are supporting authors and enabling Penguin Random House to continue to publish books for everyone. No part of this book may be used or reproduced in any manner for the purpose of training artificial intelligence technologies or systems. In accordance with Article 4(3) of the DSM Directive 2019/790, Penguin Random House expressly reserves this work from the text and data mining exception.

Designed by Bobby Birchall, Bobby&Co.
Printed and bound in Great Britain by Clays Ltd, Elcograf S.p.A.

The authorized representative in the EEA is Penguin Random House Ireland, Morrison Chambers, 32 Nassau Street, Dublin D02 YH68

A CIP catalogue record for this book is available from the British Library

ISBN: 9780857508706

Contents

Courtships 1
Situationships 27
Relationships 55

About the Author 85

Courtships

Dear Jane, How can I learn to accept a compliment? This guy I went on three dates with last year comments '🔥' on all my Stories, and all I can do is blush. How should I respond?

> *'Compliments always take you by surprise, and me never.'*

Elizabeth Bennet to her sister Jane,
PRIDE AND PREJUDICE

Dear Reader,

It is becoming to a lady to learn to accept a compliment graciously. You deserve to have your attire, manners and bearing admired, because you are a regal goddess. However, it would not be practical to thank this suitor for his '🔥' every time he bestows it upon you. Instead, make a note of it in your commonplace book and go about your day.

Your friend
Jane

Dear Jane, I have had a crush on this guy ever since I saw him play his acoustic guitar at the pub talent night. I mean, how many guys would know and like a Taylor Swift vault track? I have come back every week since to hear him play 'Watermelon Sugar', 'Good Luck, Babe!', and come close to mastering the opening riff of 'Espresso'. I know he will nail it eventually. With a work ethic like this, I can see us building a life together and achieving our goals. What should I do to make it happen?

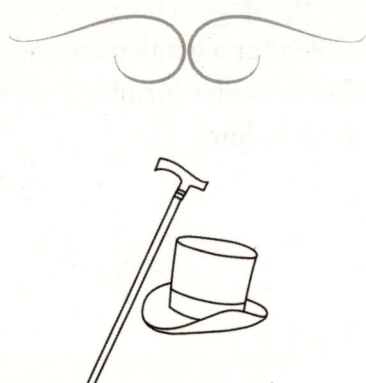

*'A lady's imagination is very rapid;
it jumps from admiration to love,
from love to matrimony,
in a moment.'*

Mr Darcy,
PRIDE AND PREJUDICE

Dear Reader,

In his defence, your beau's musical choices accord with the latest fashions. Could he possibly be considering a career on the stage? This would not be becoming for a gentleman, and you should not consider forming a serious attachment to him.

Your friend
Jane

Dear Jane, I went on a date with a really hot guy yesterday. He has a Golden Retriever puppy named after Dolly Parton, and he says he finds intelligence more attractive than a reformer Pilates body. The only problem is that he split the bill and I'm used to being taken care of. Should I wait for someone less cheap and more appreciative of my dedication to my core strength?

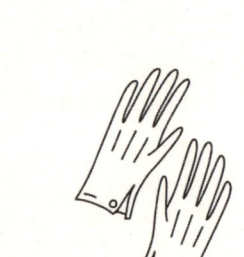

'I have no notion of people's making such a to-do about money.'

Mrs Jennings,
SENSE AND SENSIBILITY

Dear Reader,

When the bill arrives at the tea-shop, it is customary to powder one's nose for four to six minutes in the hope of the problem going away. If, however, you return to find the bill unpaid, then you must delve into your pin-money. A matter of a few pennies cannot stand between you and the company of a man with fine hunting dogs and a willingness to believe women are rational creatures.

Your friend
Jane

Dear Jane, My flatmate makes our place a total haven, cooking gorgeous meals and lighting fig-scented candles. I love her, but occasionally it would be nice to play *Minecraft*, get tortilla chip crumbs on the sofa, and bed-rot without shame. I'm planning to set her up with my co-worker, who reads poetry and re-styles his fringe a lot. Thoughts?

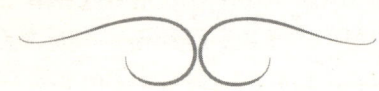

> *'Pray do not make any more matches; they are silly things, and break up one's family circle grievously.'*

Mr Woodhouse,
EMMA

Dear Reader,

It is indeed not ideal if your home is so excessively well-appointed that it highlights your own human defects and foibles. However, you seem to be unaware of the danger here: this gentleman could provide your flatmate with an ally in her aesthetic pursuits, rather than taking her for walks abroad as seems to be your intent. Consider negotiating a parlay with her: one weekend a month for you to – correct me if I have misunderstood – toil in the mines.

Your friend
Jane

D**ear Jane,** I had the weirdest date of all time yesterday. He showed up dressed in a Batman costume and insisted I call him Batman. He seemed pretty normal on the initial Hinge chat! I really want to talk about it on my channel, but I feel a bit bad calling him out so publicly. But the content! Think of the content!

> *'For what do we live, but to make sport for our neighbours, and laugh at them in our turn?'*
>
> Mr Bennet,
> **PRIDE AND PREJUDICE**

Dear Reader,

This beau cannot have been insensible of the effect his attire would have on you. I have known dandies whose top hats were so tall that they entirely blocked my view of the theatre stage. If I were to be denied the pleasure of denouncing them to my friends, I would be punished doubly. So long as this Batman has no powerful connexions in the church, you may proceed.

Your friend
Jane

Dear Jane, I'm at my wits' end with the apps. I feel like I never see anyone I like. I'm starting to adjust my expectations down/sideways. The guy who endlessly comes up in my matches and says he's 'all about the banter' is starting to look interesting. Kind of like an old friend. I'm considering letting my granny set me up with her friend's personal trainer grandson, who keeps trying to sell me protein powder. How can I persuade the algorithm to favour me?

'One's happiness must in some measure be always at the mercy of chance.'

SENSE AND SENSIBILITY

Dear Reader,

When one sits down at the card table, one can never be sure of one's hand. Even when you feel well-versed in the rules of the game, to win at cribbage is never guaranteed. To avoid losing, you must never play. If, however, you feel that you are unlikely to meet your match at the card table, there are alternatives. Visit your nearest town at a time when a company of officers has been billeted there. Drop your handkerchief outside the milliner's shop, as many times as needed before one swoops in to assist.

Your friend
Jane

Dear Jane, I feel like I've dated every kind of person – male, female, non-binary, straight, bi, pan – and I've never really fallen in love. I'm happiest spending time with my friends or grooming my Pomeranian, Pom Holland. My main dream is to win first place in a local dog show, prize £500. Am I totally weird, or is it actually best to just stay single?

'A single woman, of good fortune, is always respectable, and may be as sensible and pleasant as any body else.'

Emma,
EMMA

Dear Reader,

It sounds as if you and Pom can look forward to gaining a respectable income of five hundred a year from your endeavours. If you can fund your own establishment, the need to attract a gentleman's interest recedes greatly. Consider yourself a form of widow or other independent woman of means who can make her own choice to marry, or not as the case may be.

Your friend
Jane

Dear Jane, I've been dating for a while and I am exhausted. I cannot drink any more single espressos, hike up any more hills, or eat any more Sunday roasts at the pub. I am caffeine-intolerant, I don't like gravy, and my foot hurts. Where can I find a man who wants to sit nearby while I watch fridge organization videos all evening, then we re-set the living room and call it a night?

'One half of the world cannot understand the pleasures of the other.'

Emma,
EMMA

Dear Reader,

Your interest in improving your home through excellent management does much to commend you. I quite agree that too much society is draining. To be at home, among one's most intimate circle, is the best that life can have to offer. That we must step into the public ballroom to find a companion for this is ironic indeed. Seek out quieter corners; lurk in the bookshop rather than promenading in the street. That is where you will find your match.

Your friend
Jane

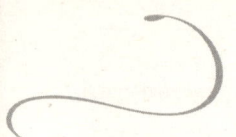

D**ear Jane**, My problem is a bit embarrassing. I'm at uni, where my mum warned me to watch out for boys, who would be throwing themselves at me at every Musical Theatre Society social. But two years in and my stack of condoms from the health centre remains untouched. Am I too hideous to love and will I be a virgin for ever?

'She had resolved at one-and-twenty to complete the sacrifice, and retire from all the pleasures of life, of rational intercourse, equal society, peace and hope.'

EMMA

Dear Reader,

Alongside an education (painting miniatures, for example, or learning a little conversational French) it is indeed important not to neglect one's marriageability. You are advanced in years, this is true. But you must not forget that a winter cold can carry off even the richest, leaving a vacancy. Be patient, continue to be seen at the Society, and trust that the right person will arrive at the right time.

Your friend
Jane

Dear Jane, Please help. There's a girl in my friendship group I've known for years, but this summer she started complimenting me on the miniature food items I make and post. She often asks for a sip of my Iced Vanilla Fudge Matcha. I find myself always wanting to sit next to her, and I also want to run my fingers through her beautiful hair and buy her Hello Kitty plushies. Any advice on how to be best friends for ever?

'I felt that I admired you, but I told myself it was only friendship.'

Edward Ferrars,
SENSE AND SENSIBILITY

Dear Reader,

Friendship is at the heart of life. Even within matrimony, you must enjoy the simple company of your mate, or facing them across the toast rack every morning will become a chore. But, while remaining within the bounds of feminine delicacy, I must add that there are types of admiration that go beyond friendship. A thoughtful gift or other act of service will always be welcomed by a lady who reciprocates your feelings. It will be natural to progress to asking for her hand.

Your friend
Jane

Dear Jane, I actually really enjoy dating, which is a blessing because I know a lot of people hate it. Where else would I get to wear my conversation-starter 'date outfit' (cat-print dress with balloon sleeves). Plus, because I'm never home, my weekly food shop has been cut in half. Girl math! But the one thing that annoys me is when the person looks really different from their pictures. Anyone with a photo more than two years old should be prosecuted by law. I mean, how hard can it be to use a recent photo?

> *'I never saw such a likeness
> in my life.'*
>
> Mr Elton,
> **EMMA**

Dear Reader,

Who among us would not be tempted to shew ourselves a little prettier or more handsome on the canvas than in life? However, if the portrait and the personage differ too drastically, the effect can be unsettling and even embarrassing. Pride can only be forgiven where there is much to be proud of. If the likeness differs to an unacceptable degree, permit yourself to say, 'La, sir, I scarce recognized you! For I expected a man of three-and-twenty, and you are as like to be his father!'

Your friend
Jane

Dear Jane, I went to Spain and had the dreamiest whirlwind holiday romance. We spent every waking hour together for ten days, but then I was forced to come home to my stupid job. He had tears in his eyes when he dropped me at the metro station. But I can see from TikTok that he's living his best life, taking tequila shots with random girls on the beach and going out every night, while I wallow in a pint of dairy-free ice cream and try to speak Spanish to the Duolingo owl. How is he able to live without me?

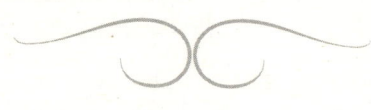

'A young man, such as you describe Mr Bingley, so easily falls in love with a pretty girl for a few weeks, and, when accident separates them, so easily forgets her.'

Mrs Gardiner,
PRIDE AND PREJUDICE

Dear Reader,

When one is away from home, for example in Bath, every sensation is heightened. A passing attachment may be formed in the ballroom that feels as if it is leading to marriage. In fact, what you see as a serious connexion may be viewed in a mere sporting light by the gentleman. You will only know it is serious if he travels to your neighbouring town and takes up residence in the finest country house therein.

Your friend
Jane

Situationships

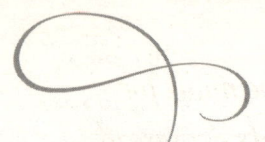

Dear Jane, The boy I've been talking to for nearly fifty-two weeks recently went for a promotion at work but didn't get it. He has stopped answering my messages, but I can see from Snapchat that he is currently in Ibiza doing jelly shots with a girl called 'missgrey'. Should I confront him while he is on holiday or wait till I pick him up from the airport?

> *'Is no allowance to be made for inadvertence, or for spirits depressed by recent disappointment?'*

Mrs Dashwood,
SENSE AND SENSIBILITY

Dear Reader,

A setback in one's career, such as failing to secure a lucrative parsonage, can be a great disappointment. A certain display of high spirits in the seedier parts of town can be permitted. But what cannot be tolerated is a failure to write. Refrain from messaging further; glance not upon the Snapchat. Consider your engagement broken and enjoy the sympathy of your friends.

Your friend
Jane

Dear Jane, I'm considering making my situationship official. Except this would mean introducing him to my friends. On his socials he has one classy black-and-white self-portrait and like a thousand pictures of trees. But in real life he's kind of . . . rough around the edges. More of a 'grab me a beer' lad who swears at people who beat him on *Halo* than a thoughtful poetic lover-boy. How can I PR this situation so they'll accept and love him like I do?

> *'I have no pleasure in seeing my friends, unless I can believe myself fit to be seen.'*

Frank Churchill,
EMMA

Dear Reader,

Your peevish betrothed sounds like he has spent too much time at sea. Although quadrille or bridge can indeed raise hot tempers, his conduct is too odious for mixed company. You must trust in the affection of your friends to withstand potential assaults on their sensibilities. If he proves too vulgar, you must cultivate connexions with those who bring wit to the conversation. And if not wit, then sense. And if sense cannot be got, we will settle for silence.

Your friend
Jane

Dear Jane, My crush is like Jekyll and Hyde, I think. Is Jekyll a cute guy who always texts back and Hyde is weird and cold? I should probably read that book. Anyway. He sends me all his favourite memes and laughs at mine. He says, 'Good morning, angel,' every single day. But when I see him IRL, he's like a different person who barely knows me. He goes all red and doesn't show me any special affection. How can I make these two different boys become one, and make that one my boyfriend?

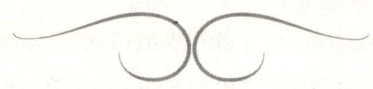

> *'I am so foolishly shy, that I often seem negligent, when I am only kept back by my natural awkwardness.'*
>
> Edward Ferrars,
> **SENSE AND SENSIBILITY**

Dear Reader,

Your beau has been infected by that illness most destructive to love: reticence, fear, shyness! The version of you he writes to lives only in his imaginings. Suddenly to find the real you in his wealthy aunt's second-best parlour is a shock to his composure. You must have the confidence to bridge the two situations. Take a turn about the room, and as you pass him, make some reference to his 'favourite meme'. He will understand immediately that you are, for example, making sport of the Kool-Aid Man breaking through a wall (the wall of his shyness).

Your friend
Jane

Dear Jane, I've been dating someone for three months and it's crunch time. He texts back 90 per cent of the time, always pays on dates, and most importantly, we both watch reality TV. I'm not in love with him, but I'm scared if I break up with him I'll have to go back on the apps. I am dreading having to summarize the last seven seasons of *The Real Housewives of Beverly Hills* to another love interest. Should I just stick it out?

> *'If a woman doubts as to whether she should accept a man or not, she certainly ought to refuse him.'*
>
> Emma,
> **EMMA**

Dear Reader,

For once I am able to answer unequivocally. You must not accept this man's proposal. We cannot be ruled only by our hearts but they, too, must have their say in the matter of our marriage. Shared interests and mutual dislikes are indeed a boon to domestic felicity. But this merely allows you to occupy the same parlour at the same time without argument. The same effect could be achieved with an absorbing embroidery project and a well-trained spaniel.

Your friend
Jane

Dear Jane, I have been seeing my crush for five months. I am totally head over heels with him. The last two months have been torture, trying not to shout 'I LOVE YOU' in his face when he wakes up. Or smiles at me. Or does anything at all. He hasn't given me any sign of feeling the same way, such as planning romantic escapades or gazing at me for long periods. On Valentine's Day, he gave me a fist bump and a half-eaten box of caramel truffles he got from work. What do I do?

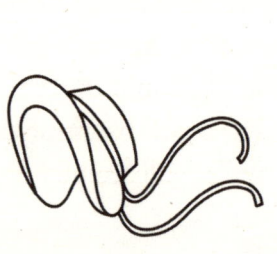

> *'My feelings will not be repressed.
> You must allow me to tell you how
> ardently I admire and love you.'*

Mr Darcy,
PRIDE AND PREJUDICE

Dear Reader,

I commend you on your five months of feigning serenity despite your inner turmoil. I assume that you have given the gentleman some shy smiles and perhaps even some teasing laughter and flattery. Has your sister intervened? If this is the case and you see no result, you may need to resort to the following. With trembling lip say, 'Sir, if I had not more sense I should think myself quite in love with you!' He must then either propose or take leave of you for ever.

Your friend
Jane

Dear Jane, It was my birthday yesterday. I threw a carefully curated party at the local brewery, which is within walking distance of the guy I've been sort of seeing. I sent a three-week, two-week, one-week and day-of reminder to the group chat. He never showed up. I don't even like beer. Why wouldn't he come? Should I have booked the vegan brunch place directly below his flat instead?

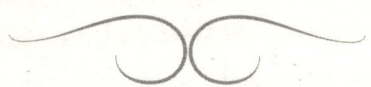

'I dare say he might come if he would.'

Mr Knightley,
EMMA

Dear Reader,

It is true that a chill can strike at any time, especially if this gentleman has been riding to hounds or partaking of outdoor waters. But to believe that a man would fail to attend the party of his particular favourite without being in life-threatening danger is not possible. You have curated a most pleasant occasion that suits his sensibilities and left many visiting cards as reminders. It is beyond doubt: he has spurned you.

Your friend
Jane

D**ear Jane,** Bit of a weird one. There's this guy at work who I absolutely loathe. He glowers at me in meetings, ignores me at work drinks, and is constantly in the office kitchen when I'm trying to get a mini Diet Coke. He's tall and has these broad shoulders so he's completely in the way. The weirdest thing of all is that I swear I saw him adding cans to my DC stash. I constantly think about how annoying he is while sipping from my now inexhaustible supply of drinks. I . . . don't know what my question is.

'That would be the greatest misfortune of all! To find a man agreeable whom one is determined to hate!'

Elizabeth Bennet,
PRIDE AND PREJUDICE

Dear Reader,

Some people enter your life like a ray of spring sunshine through a south-facing parlour window. Others appear like a rain cloud over the walk you were forced to take after being denied use of the carriage by your unfeeling father. It is one of life's greatest surprises that love can follow regardless of first impressions. Keep your mind open to possibilities and enjoy your abundance of cordials.

Your friend
Jane

Dear **Jane**, I have met a really nice boy and I am absolutely smitten. After a string of guys who only wanted to come round at 1 a.m., I have the opposite problem for once: he wants to do constant cute dates. If it's not an exhibition of my favourite anime artists, it's a pop-up juicery where they mix you a drink based on your sun, moon and rising signs. Now he wants to go and see the Northern Lights! I can't afford all this, or the appropriate outfits. How do I subtly get him to tone down the endless life-enriching magic without pouring cold water on his whimsy?

'Where there is affection young people are seldom withheld, by immediate want of fortune, from entering into engagements with each other.'

Elizabeth Bennet,
PRIDE AND PREJUDICE

Dear Reader,

Poverty is a major problem for forming an attachment. If one has but a little money, the public mail coach can be taken instead of a carriage and four. Last year's bonnet can be re-trimmed at little cost. One must cut one's cloth accordingly. You must seize the reins of organization from this most avid coachman. Before he can make suggestions, fill his calendar with so many walks around the park that there is no time for voyages by sea.

Your friend
Jane

Dear Jane, I am deep in the situationship trenches. Every time I get close to falling in love, they do something to give me the ick and I am compelled to never text them again. How can I love a man who changes the bin bag in a weird way or licks his yoghurt lid? Once the ick icketh it cannot be un-icked, you know? I dream of meeting someone passionate and mysterious who will never be boring and annoying.

> *'I have no notion of loving people by halves; it is not my nature. My attachments are always excessively strong.'*

Isabella Thorpe,
NORTHANGER ABBEY

Dear Reader,

You sound governed more by sensibility than sense. For girls with an active imagination and an enjoyment of Romantic landscapes, the ordinary and domestic will never suffice. I suggest that during the next rainstorm, you roam the moors until you meet a soul with a similar inability to tolerate the domestic, and you can die in each other's arms after catching a highly avoidable chill.

Your friend
Jane

Dear Jane, I hooked up with this guy from a karaoke bar after we both picked 'Hallelujah' by Leonard Cohen and now I can't stop thinking of our future kitten, which we will name Leonard in honour of our origin story. From my research, I have found out his mother's stepsister's goddaughter is getting married in the church down my road on Sunday. What if I pretend to be a parishioner, just so we can bump into each other on the day? I would enjoy singing the hymns at least.

*'Artlessness will never
do in love matters.'*

Lady Susan,
LADY SUSAN

Dear Reader,

Trusting to fate can only lead to spinsterhood. The betrothed couples you see falling so easily and naturally into engagements will have benefited from meddling mamas, wealthy relatives to throw convenient balls, and diplomatic sisters who are willing to vacate the parlour when the gentleman calls. A little artfulness is sometimes needed. By all means contrive the peril you speak of, but perhaps it is the greatest peril of all you must confront: honesty about your feelings.

Your friend
Jane

Dear Jane, So I've been sleeping with my ex. I know, I know, but the vibes are better when we are together but not together and I know deep down we still love each other. I was scrolling through Instagram and saw a girl soft-launch her guy without showing his face. The shape of this man's hand looks strangely similar to my ex's, which I saw just two nights ago wrestling the TV remote from me so I am sure I am not mistaken. Do I call him out or walk away?

'They had no conversation together, no intercourse but what the commonest civility required. Once so much to each other! Now nothing!'

PERSUASION

Dear Reader,

It is a simple fact that if one is engaged, even in secret, one cannot accept other, more advantageous offers of marriage. While you remain in an understanding with this gentleman, you will be unable to look around you for suitable bachelors. As he already considers your engagement dissolved, a short letter to bid him adieu will suffice to release him. You will then industriously apply yourself to gaining invitations to balls and weekend parties.

Your friend
Jane

Dear Jane, I am a nice person. I pride myself on being friendly and bubbly. I got voted 'Most Likely to Lend You Their Car' at school. It just makes me feel good helping others! But when it comes to dating, this is a problem. I say yes to dates, even with people I'm not sure about. Last week, I ended up pet-sitting a very aggressive chihuahua whilst my date made chicken sashimi. I had to ring up the GP at 8 a.m. the next day to inspect a bite from that tiny dog, and I am mildly convinced I have food poisoning. My friends say I'm a doormat. How do I find a balance?

> *'I am not fond of the idea of my shrubberies being always approachable.'*

Sir Walter,
PERSUASION

Dear Reader,

You have confused the appearance of a kind heart and generous temperament with the reality of one. Charity towards our inferiors is a virtue. But where is your charity towards yourself? If you spend so much time bestowing favours upon others, you will neglect your own hearth. Beginning immediately, cancel your social engagements and retreat to your cottage. Only the most honoured of guests will henceforth be allowed in. Furthermore, be cautious of other people's pets. They can disturb even the most refined of tempers.

Your friend
Jane

Dear Jane, I've had a crush on my closest male friend for as long as I can remember. Now he's getting married, which I did not see coming! I dread having to make the best woman speech at his wedding, pretending to be happy for him when really I want to rip the veil off her head and shriek, 'It should have been me!' He's hinting that I should hook up with his best man, just because we're both single. How can I get through this and demolish the crush for ever?

> *'Where the heart is really attached,
> I know very well how little one can be
> pleased with the attention of any body else.'*

Isabella,
NORTHANGER ABBEY

Dear Reader,

Some of us are destined to nurse a single attachment all our lives, never wavering despite all the signs being against it. Make a gracious speech with no mention of ripping off veils but plentiful reference to your own exciting travel plans, for example to Lyme Regis. Wave them off on their honeymoon. Then dedicate yourself to a programme of invigorating walks in the fresh air until you are too tired to think about him. Avoidance of his company is the only remedy.

Your friend
Jane

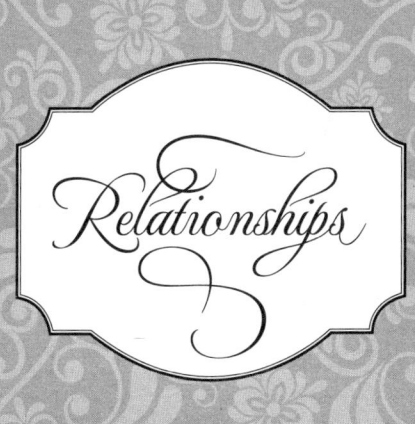

Dear Jane, This year I swore off dating after my boyfriend broke up with me to become a full-time podcaster. Apparently he couldn't record with me 'constantly laughing in the background'. To prove a point, I spent a week at a silent retreat getting in touch with my authentic self and taking shrooms. I met someone there after my hot yoga class, and today we have decided to make it official. My friends say I am delusional. How can I persuade them that it's not too soon?

'Seven years would be insufficient to make some people acquainted with each other, and seven days are more than enough for others.'

Marianne Dashwood,
SENSE AND SENSIBILITY

Dear Reader,

As you know from your previous, long-term understanding with a gentleman, you can spend the better part of a decade sitting next to someone on the chaise and never quite know them. Neither seven days nor seven years is enough time until you develop the sense to see them as they really are, not as you would like them to be. Find contentment in your present situation, and do not neglect to express your disfavour on his podcast review page.

Your friend
Jane

Dear Jane, I am mortified! I just got dumped by being tagged in a picture of him and his real girlfriend, a very gorgeous bookfluencer who I actually support on Patreon. I thought I had met the perfect guy who had read all the same books as me, but now I suspect he was just repeating her (immaculate) opinions. I should have known that he'd never read *Little Women* after I said my favourite character was Jo March, and he said, 'Yeah, I love him.' How do I ever recover?

'When pain is over, the remembrance of it often becomes a pleasure.'

Anne Elliot,
PERSUASION

Dear Reader,

Disappointment in love is a most vexatious experience. The possibility of meeting with the gentleman at a musical gathering, or while taking a turn in the park, is too probable for comfort. However, you must not retreat from the world. In a twelvemonth, you may be able to remember your time together with a certain fondness. Ideally, this will be from within the security of a new, better relationship, while he suffers one broken engagement after another before declaring bankruptcy.

Your friend
Jane

Dear Jane, How do I find a hobby my partner and I can share? They like mixed martial arts and tending to their orchids with a pair of tiny scissors. My only hobby is creating custom Sims of boyband members whilst watching old sitcoms in bed. We never spend time together!

'I could not be happy with a man whose taste did not in every point coincide with my own.'

Marianne Dashwood,
SENSE AND SENSIBILITY

Dear Reader,

I assure you there is a world of pastimes yet to be explored. If you both take up the pianoforte, you can spend your time together much more pleasantly and afford entertainment at every party. Before long, you will wonder why you differed in your interests at all.

Your friend
Jane

Dear Jane, I have been in the talking stage for over a month now with someone I met online. He has asked me to be his girlfriend using a string of twenty-six emojis referencing all our in-jokes (for example, helicopter, door, winky face), culminating in the sparkle heart. I was SOMF (swept off my feet). Should I say yes based on the chats alone? We have yet to meet IRL.

'A woman is not to marry a man merely because she is asked, or because he is attached to her, and can write a tolerable letter.'

Emma,
EMMA

Dear Reader,

The mind may be diverted through a clever turn of phrase, or good knowledge of the latest gossip from Bath. But the heart cannot truly be engaged without laying eyes on the subject. Without intimate knowledge of bearing, height and the crispness of his shirting, you would be a fool to commit yourself.

Your friend
Jane

Dear Jane, I've been with my partner for two years. We get along well in every way; for example, we like the same setting on the thermostat and leaving concerts before the encore so we can get ahead of the crowds. When we are at a restaurant, he takes the pickles out of my burger and I eat the olives off his salad. Yet, sometimes, I wonder if there's more to life. Should I ditch him and see what (and who) else is out there?

'Sense will always have attractions for me.'

Elinor Dashwood,
SENSE AND SENSIBILITY

Dear Reader,

Much depends on what you want from life. A man of reasonable income, and who is pleasing both at a recital and in his own parlour, has much to recommend him. This man seems skilled indeed at moderation, and you say that you are of like mind. There may be more to life, but is there more to you?

Your friend
Jane

Dear Jane, I'm a big fan of those Christmas movies where a city girl travels to a small town and finds her soulmate chopping wood near the inn. I've been with my boyfriend for four years now and I make sure all our holidays are to places with autumnal leaves, babbling brooks, waterfalls, and other romantic outdoor proposal locations. My nails are done at all times, so much so that I think my nail tech has started to avoid booking me because she's bored of doing French tips. I'm starting to think marriage isn't on his mind but it's something I really want, big proposal and all.

'It is a truth universally acknowledged, that a single man in possession of a good fortune, must be in want of a wife.'

PRIDE AND PREJUDICE

Dear Reader,

Your patience and planning are admirable. The "____shire" Company of Officers would benefit from a captain like you, if ladies had professional occupations. You are quite right in laying the groundwork for his offer. All but the most confident or deluded gentlemen need strong assurance that their proposal will be accepted. To delay for four years, however, must give you pause. Perhaps he is a second or even third son to a baronet and will not inherit the title, forcing him to seek an income before he can marry? Discover his reason and then you can plan your next campaign.

Your friend
Jane

Dear Jane, My partner is being really jealous and annoying. I have a co-worker I may have mentioned a couple of times. We both watched *Friends* for the first time recently so obviously have to discuss the Ross/Rachel situation. He also sugar crashes at 3 p.m. and needs a sweet treat, so we go for gluten-free cookies together most days. How can I persuade my partner that he is my one and only and this guy is just a friend? I mean an actual friend, not a Friend I will eventually fall in love with.

'The imaginations of other people will carry them away to form wrong judgments of our conduct, and to decide on it by slight appearances.'

SENSE AND SENSIBILITY

Dear Reader,

Your new acquaintance sounds most diverting – a handsome gentleman willing to sit and converse about one's friends is a rare find. However, your fiancé should distinguish between flirtation and serious attachment. As you could not break off your engagement without damaging your own honour, he should trust that any wrongdoing is entirely his own fancy.

Your friend
Jane

Dear Jane, My partner and I love to snuggle up and watch TV on Friday nights. We are two thirds of the way through *Cook to the Death*, the K-drama where you have to cook a perfect dish to avoid being killed. I had one Friday night out with the girls and he watched the rest of the series without me. He says he is sorry but he couldn't resist. I have never felt more betrayed.

> *'We always know when we are acting wrong.'*
>
> Marianne Dashwood,
> SENSE AND SENSIBILITY

Dear Reader,

To snatch up the latest periodical and secretly discover the end to a story before your beloved has returned from the milliner is an offence, but a pardonable one. Your husband's primary and most unnecessary mistake was in failing to keep the secret of his crime. I can only assume you have been married less than a twelve-month. I assure you, he will not risk such transparency again.

Your friend
Jane

Dear Jane, My stupid oaf of a boyfriend has really hurt my feelings. I was getting dressed (in a Premier Inn, at 7.30 a.m.) for his sister's wedding and I asked him how I looked, expecting compliments on my slinky maxi dress, or my beachy waves, or my teeny-tiny handbag. He barely looked up from his 'how to tie a bow-tie' video and said I looked 'fine'. Why did I bother?? I'm now home, wearing my teddy-bear PJs and seething.

> '*It would be mortifying to the feelings of many ladies, could they be made to understand how little the heart of man is affected by what is costly or new in their attire.*'
>
> NORTHANGER ABBEY

Dear Reader,

I sympathize. A lady will take hours over her toilette, selecting her finest muslin and tonging her hair into ringlets, only for the gentleman to compliment her on her natural beauty, as if one simply rose from slumber looking like this. If indeed they compliment you at all. To expect them to match our knowledge and skill in this realm will only lead to distress. Exchange compliments with other ladies, who will satisfy you by envying the hairdressing techniques of your maid, and wishing to know the address of your hatmaker.

Your friend
Jane

Dear Jane, I'm the bad guy in this story. My boyfriend and I love to roast each other in the name of comedy, but I took things too far: I made a joke about him being a redhead in front of his friends. They have renamed their group chat 'Three Men and a Carrot', and constantly call him a 'half-pint of ginger beer' and ask him for directions to Gingerbread Lane. He does not find it funny. How can I make it up to him?

> *'As his composure convinced her that all was safe, her wit flowed along.'*
>
> **PRIDE AND PREJUDICE**

Dear Reader,

It appears that you and your betrothed have been walking a fine line for some time. When we become comfortable with sharp words or gossip, it is only a matter of time until we draw blood where we did not intend to. As you have both been drawing the blades of wit, perhaps it is time to call a truce. He has entered into a duel of words and lost. As an act of kindness, retire your weapons and leave the humorous comments to the gentlemen at his club.

Your friend
Jane

Dear Jane, I just broke up with my long-term boyfriend, who was also my first love. Don't worry, I'm fine! I just don't know how to date, where to live, and have been listening to Adele on repeat for the last three weeks. All my future plans were with him and the last time I dated I was, like, fifteen years old. I tried to flirt with the handsome guy who gets on the same train carriage every morning, but when I opened my mouth, nothing came out. I just gaped at him like a koi fish. He looked so confused, then quietly asked me if there was someone he could call to help me. I can't remember how to flirt with someone, let alone fall in love with them. Am I doomed?

*'The worn-out past was sunk
in the freshness of what was coming.'*

EMMA

Dear Reader,

You are embarking on a significant journey. When one is disappointed in love, there are three possibilities to look forward to. Firstly, you may die a spinster. Secondly, you may find your way back to your previous betrothed; consider walking out often in Bath. Thirdly, you may gain a little wisdom and find yourself, even at the age of perhaps seven-and-twenty – or beyond! – able to form a new connexion with someone you would not previously have liked, or found worthy.

Your friend
Jane

Dear Jane, When I met my boyfriend, I fell for him immediately. We're very happy and I've introduced him to my friends. They all got on great, but on the way home one of my mates texted me saying he looks exactly like my ex. In fact he said, 'like your ex but not as hot'. I compared their profile pics and, oh my god, they could be twins! The other night, I almost slipped up and called him my ex's name. I wish my friend had never pointed this out to me. What should I do?

> *'One man's ways may be as good as another's, but we all like our own best.'*
>
> Admiral Croft,
> **PERSUASION**

Dear Reader,

We each have a particular fancy when it comes to a gentleman's looks. Some prefer hair of a lighter tint, some a darker. Some prefer a shy man whose utterances are thoughtful, while others prefer a voice that booms across the ballroom. There is no accounting for taste. Once one has been out in society for a few years, you notice that there are only so many types of person. You must choose the type you like, and friends be damned.

Your friend
Jane

Dear Jane, I have just started a new job as a tree surgeon. On my first day, I was walking through the woods and bumped into a geologist. I couldn't believe it — it was The One That Got Away. We met in the rainforest while travelling in our gap years but lost touch at uni. At the time, I thought we were just too different. I have thought about him regretfully so often since then. Do you think there's such a thing as second chances?

'You pierce my soul. I am half agony, half hope. Tell me not that I am too late, that such precious feelings are gone for ever.'

Captain Wentworth,
PERSUASION

Dear Reader,

In our little lives we experience so few real chances. We walk from house to village and back again. We dine with our neighbours and play at cards. The luckiest among us are able to marry well enough to remain near our sisters. Your luck seems to be of a rare kind. Walk out again immediately, and feign a fall upon some rocks to show that you embrace his interests in a way you did not before. When he has concluded his inspection of the rocks, he will surely come to your aid. Then you can tell him how you feel.

Your friend
Jane

D**ear Jane**, I've been with my boyfriend basically since the beginning of time. We met at school and were each other's first everything. My friends all have hilarious stories like dating a guy who showed up dressed as Batman, while they call me 'the old married lady' just because I have 'Ben's girlfriend, mum to 2 🐶' in my Insta bio. I'm happy and I love him, and the Labradoodles, but I wonder if I should have gathered some more interesting stories before settling down so young?

> *'If adventures will not befall a young lady in her own village, she must seek them abroad.'*

NORTHANGER ABBEY

Dear Reader,

What great fortune has befallen you! You have never experienced anxiety about empty slots on your dance card, or hovered by the milliner's window hoping an officer will approach you. How your single friends over the age of one-and-twenty must envy you. However, it is true that you have been shut out of the delightful agonies of romance. In order to have the best of both worlds, consider writing your imaginary romantic adventures down in the form of a book.

Your friend
Jane

Satu Hämeenaho-Fox is an Elizabeth Bennett with a Marianne Dashwood rising. She is an author of books about culture and celebrity, including Taylor Swift, Harry Styles, Zendaya and Lady Gaga. She has also written several children's books on art and fashion history for New York's Metropolitan Museum of Art.

Thanks to Jess, Sam and Ralph for their help with this book.